A Walk Up
The Mountain

Produced by Daniel Weiss Associates, Inc.
33 West 17 Street, New York, NY 10011

Text copyright © 1990 Daniel Weiss Associates, Inc.,
and Al Jarnow

Illustration copyright © Freya Tanz

Published by Silver Press, a division of
Silver Burdett Press, Inc., Simon & Schuster, Inc.
Prentice Hall Bldg., Englewood Cliffs, NJ 07632
For information address: Silver Press.

Printed in the United States of America
10 9 8 7 6 5 4 3 2 1

Library of Congress Cataloging-in-Publication Data
Arnold, Caroline.
A walk up the mountain/written by Caroline Arnold;
illustrated by Freya Tanz.
A Ap. cm.—(First facts)
Summary: Describes the geographic features of mountains, plants
and animals that live there, and how to climb mountains.
1. Mountain ecology—Juvenile literature. [1. Mountains.]
I. Tanz, Freya, ill. II. Title. III. Series: First facts
(Englewood Cliffs, N.J.)
QH541.5.M65A76   90-8405
1990574.5.264—dc20   CIP
                                                          AC
ISBN 0-671-68667-4   ISBN 0-671-68663-1 (lib. bdg.)

First Facts™

A Walk Up The Mountain

Written by Caroline Arnold
Illustrated by Freya Tanz

Silver Press

Up, up, up!
Every step will take you higher and higher.
Listen to the wind whoosh through the pines.
Feel the cool breeze on your face.
Where are we?
We're at the bottom of a mountain.
Let's walk to the top.

Cedar, birch, and pines grow tall
on low mountain slopes.
The bluejay has found an acorn.
It uses its sharp beak
to break open seeds and nuts.
The chickadee is hungry too.

On higher slopes, only pine trees grow.
It's cold and windy up here.
Look at the pine trees on this ridge.
See how the strong winds have bent their
trunks and branches all to one side.

Watch the eagle soar over the trees.
Caw, caw, cry the crows.
We're so high we can see over
the treetops, too.
We are above the timber line.

Look at this rock wall.
Can you see all the different layers?
Each one took a long time to form.
Sometimes pieces of the earth tip up,
or slide across each other.
This happens so slowly that you
can't see it.

Oops! It's starting to rain.
Along with snow, ice, and wind,
rain wears down the surface of rocks.
It helps make rough edges smooth.
Old mountains have rounded tops.
Newer mountains are jagged.
Can you tell if this mountain is old or new?
It takes millions of years for
mountains to form.
And it takes millions of years
to wear them down again.

Cracked
Shield
Lichen

Red Capped Lichen

Few plants can grow on solid rock.
Feel this rough patch.
It's a plant called lichen.
Lichens cling to rocks.
Some are greenish gray.
Others are yellow or orange.
When lichens die, they rot and crumble.
They make new soil where other
mountain plants can grow.

Yellow
Map
Lichen

Mountain flowers bloom in the rocky soil.

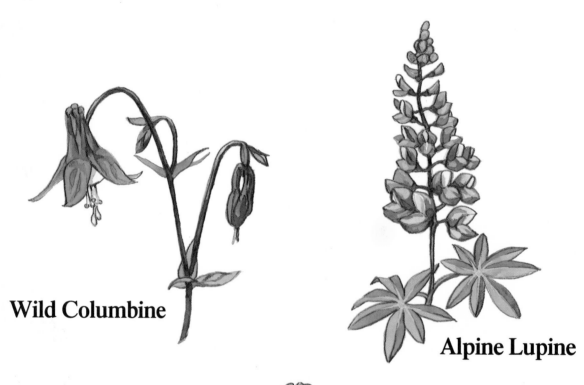

Wild Columbine

Alpine Lupine

Moss Campion

What's that coming toward you?
It's a pika.
Pikas cut grass with their teeth,
and leave it to dry in the sun.
Then pikas store the grass,
so they have food when winter comes.

Who's that whistling?
It's a marmot on the alert.
It whistles to let other marmots
know that danger is near.

Mountain goats live
above the timber line, too.
Their long hair keeps them warm.
And their sturdy feet help them
to leap and climb on narrow ledges.

What's that white patch ahead?
Brr! It's snow.
Tall mountain peaks almost
always have snow on them.

Drip, drip, drip.
Melting snow trickles to the ground and
forms a stream.
Watch the water race over the rocks.

Look over there!
The glacier glitters in the sun.
A glacier is packed snow that has turned to ice.
It slides slowly down the mountain—
just a few inches a year.
It pushes stones and dirt in front of it.
Over thousands of years,
glaciers carve out mountain valleys.

Expert climbers sometimes go up
steep cliffs to get to the top of a
tall mountain.
They use strong ropes, axes, spikes,
and special shoes to keep them from slipping.

But you don't need to be an expert climber
to have fun on a mountain.
In winter, you can ski or snowshoe.
In summer, you can hike or fish.

There are mountains all over the world.

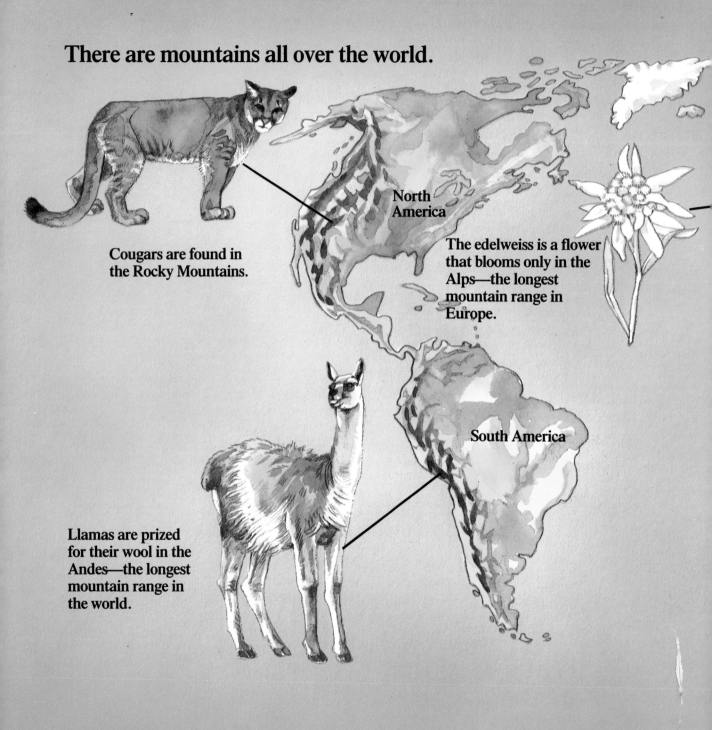

North America

Cougars are found in the Rocky Mountains.

The edelweiss is a flower that blooms only in the Alps—the longest mountain range in Europe.

South America

Llamas are prized for their wool in the Andes—the longest mountain range in the world.

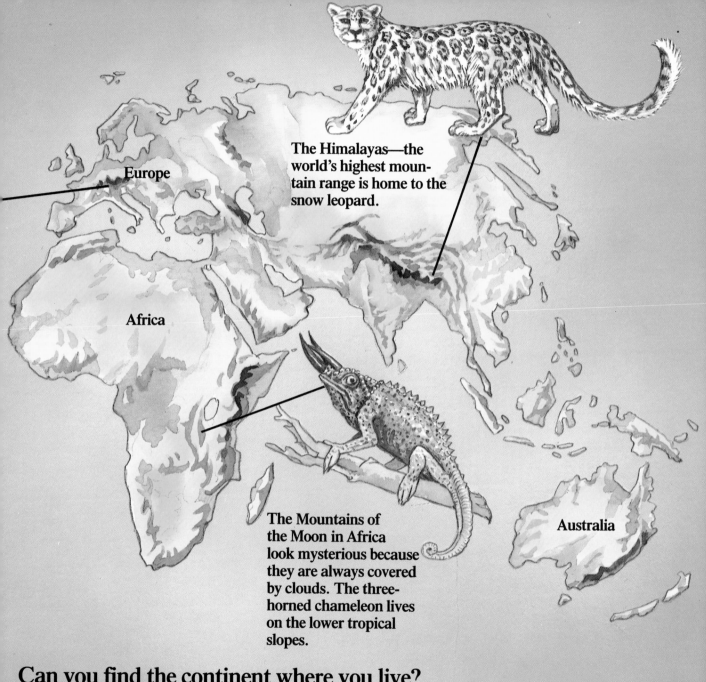

Europe

The Himalayas—the world's highest mountain range is home to the snow leopard.

Africa

The Mountains of the Moon in Africa look mysterious because they are always covered by clouds. The three-horned chameleon lives on the lower tropical slopes.

Australia

Can you find the continent where you live?
Which mountain is closest to you?

What did you see on your way up the mountain?
Here are some clues to help you remember.
Can you name each one?